The Evil California
Franchise Tax Board

by Adrian Vance

© 2014 by Adrian Vance

Introduction

This is the story of people who have been, and continue to be, intimidated and robbed by the California Franchise Tax Board with the aid of banks charging customers exorbitant fees for "legal services." They are anything, but legal and many banks will not collaborate in these crimes.

Some banks take funds from Social Security Benefit accounts, which is not permitted. If the depositor knows the law they can insist funds be returned and they will be, but why must a citizen have to ask for a law to be observed by a California Tax Board and a bank? Such transfers are grand theft.

We presented evidence to the California State Attorney General and she told us that she could do nothing! It is her job to defend the California Franchise Tax Board against me! When I asked who oversaw the board I was told it was the Governor. It took several letters and phone calls to get action from the Governor's office, but it finally happened and I appear to have prevailed. The California Franchise Tax Board will never fully resolve a matter with a letter saying they are satisfied. This is the attitude of a bureau gone rogue.

They are never satisfied. This is an evil bureau, as you will see when you read the many accounts we have collected thanks to Stephen Frank's blog, "California Politics." That one blog could pull hundreds of stories of the kind you will read means there are thousands more of such cases. The California Franchise Tax board has become a criminal enterprise.

This book is meant to inspire the Governor of California to investigate and prosecute the criminals in this bureau. Barring that action, we need a legal foundation to file a class action. We only ask that our Constitutions and laws be enforced and all who have been damaged by the California Franchise Tax Board be made whole and compensated for mistreatment.

Contents

Introduction

Adrian Vance case history

The Blog Responses

And

Comments

Preface

This document is specifically prepared to read on the air in a talk show format. All materials in the Response and Comment sections have been edited for misspelled words, sentence fragments and grammar errors to preserve the content and intent of the writer to the most accurate degree we can accomplish. In 90% of the cases the blog inputs are totally unchanged. No deliberate content alterations were made.

There is enough material on these pages to fill an entire week of one hour, commercial broadcast programming without calls. We do not recommend using this for a full week, but perhaps present sections of it over a month or six weeks. This is material that will inspire call-ins and will likely produce more people who have had these experiences.

We recommend that anyone who has been subjected to an FTB assault contact the California FTB Advocacy Unit as they have a group within the bureau that defends the taxpayer and they seem genuine. This adds to the mystery of the situation as it forces the idea that the California Franchise Tax Board is either a schizophrenic bureau or there is a rogue unit within that is operating in a manner not consistent with bureau policy or guidelines. To be sure this is a puzzle wrapped in an enigma sealed in a bureau. May we be the people that will sort this out and find justice in the effort. Too many people have too long been seriously harmed by the actions of the California Franchise Tax Board.

The Beginning

I filed my state income for the year 2007 in April 2008, per law, and without thinking much about it included a short note regarding a flaw in the state's instructions regarding deductions. They had called for the subtraction of a negative number at one point. The right set of numbers could cost the state a lot of money if those instructions were followed in accord with the laws of mathematics and the rules of grammar. My correction was but a few easily understood, helpful to the state sentences, so thought I…

If I expected anything it would have been a nice thank-you note, but two years later I received a dun, with a healthy fine and an interest penalty for unpaid taxes, but would be considered usury under the law so I went to my 2007 record files, having learned to keep everything, and there I found the Franchise Tax Board, FTB, had not cashed my check. I had not noticed as it was at the time I converted to on-line banking and was no longer resolving my account every month as it was updated by the bank automatically every day. I had gotten into the habit of logging in every few days, paying most of my bills on line and dealing with problems immediately. The FTB check simply went out-of-mind.

I called the FTB, got a young man on the phone, explained it to him and he agreed that where the return had passed "No Check Included" checkpoint they must have lost it after that, and while it would have been nice if I had caught it, that was not really my obligation, they should have not waited two years so he said, "Just send us a check for the tax." I did and thought that was the end of it as there was no further explanation in the dun.

In a few months the same notice arrived again! I called the Franchise Tax Board and this time was told that my 2007 Federal Income Tax return had shown a $10,500 higher income than that I had reported to California! I said, "Not possible, send me what you received from the IRS and I will straighten it out. There must be some mistake."

"I can't do that," said the female voice on the phone, that is illegal."

"Since when is it illegal to send me official information regarding my taxes?" I asked.
"That's the law," insisted she and this conversation went around and around that single point until I finally gave up. At this point it was clear to me I was dealing with disingenuous people and perhaps a roque, out-of-control bureau. Having had experience with both I knew better than to appeal to the administration of the bureau as they are always directing such actions. Nothing happens inside a government bureau that is not endorsed by the people at the top. They know what is going on to the

last paper clip purchase. I wrote letters documenting my case to my state Senator and Assemblyman. In a few days I heard from their people and they seemed to be in motion, but nothing happened as they were ameliorated by Franchise Tax Board people who gave them other phone numbers I could call. I called the numbers and got nowhere. I was only asking to see what they had received from the IRS as that was the problem. One conversation I had told the story:

I asked the lady on the line if I could get a copy of whatever the IRS had sent to the FTB, telling her I had been told by a person in my Senator's office that it was legal. There was a long pause after that and she came back saying, "You can't read the record." "What do you mean?" I asked. "It's magnetic," she responded. "How do you see it?" asked I. "On a computer screen," answered she. "OK, look on your keyboard for the 'Print Screen' key, press it and send me what comes out." There were a few seconds of silence and then a loud "click." She hung up!

I called my contacts in the Assemblyman's and Senator's office. The first was appalled, but gave little more than sympathy saying she would continue to work on it and the second, a man, was sympathetic and also told me that he had noted the FTB had sent me the first notice six months after the statute of limitations had expired! I called the FTB legal department and the answer was "So what?" That confirmed I was dealing with rogue bureau out to get money by whatever means they could, owed or not; legal or not.

I called the Attorney General's office only to be told they could not help me as they were obliged to defend the FTB. When asked who oversees them I had to wait several days to be told "The Governor." So I contacted his office and spoke with a very amenable young man, sent a letter and soon got a letter back that was polite, but noncommittal. Nonetheless, I had opened that door. This exchange of letters and phone calls went on for three years until I finally got enough documents from the IRS to make my case in a way that a child could understand with records that were all veriafiable. One lady in the FTB Advocates office agreed with me saying she would have to send it someone in the bureau to finally resolve the matter and I would hear from them anon. I am still waiting years later and after letters asking for a final resolution document.The posts following were all to Stephen Frank's blog "California Politics" in response to a short piece I ran there. Stephan has worked in Sacramento for an Assemblyman and published a newsletter as well as his blog. He has about 40,000 readers a day. That we have received over 100 responses of this kind from that sample says there are many more such cases and where they are from all over the nation the base is 318 million so the potential is possibly 800,000 such cases and where they are seeking one to several thousand Dollars in every case we are talking about billions of Dollars with most of it stolen.

Note: California Taxpayers Advocates Office and their number is 800-883-5910, FAX 916-855-2101

The blog responses and "Note" commentaries follow:

"Anonymous:

Something needs to be done about the fraud and corruption being done by the California FTB....they have stolen money from my bank account twice without notifying me or due process. Class action lawsuit? Anyone who has been victimized by the FTB, please post so we can get this ball rolling."

"Guest

Just victimized last week. I live in Oregon. Moved from California in late May, 2000. Never received anything from them. Never had notice of a lien. They said that because I held a Real Estate License in the year 2000 and didn't file a CA return in 2000 they assessed me a tax based upon the average income of a real estate professional in CA in 2000. That average was $45,000! They took my SS, my little savings account, and part of the support from my husband. I am frantic to say the least!

Note: The FTB not only collected money in another state, in violation of the Federal Constitution, but took Social Security money, in violation of "Section 207" of the SSI Code and taking money without notice is always illegal and handled the matter as if we were under Napoleonic law, which we are not.

Marilyn

"Me too! Last week they took $1,570.00 without notification. Nothing .Just Poof and all of my money is gone. I need to pay rent. I need to buy medication and food. I never worked in California. I am in shock."

Note: Again, no notification, no court action, no correspondence, no identification, just a person with, in this case, "the wrong name!" This is police state activity appropriate to Nazi Germany, Communist East Germany or North Korea, not America; and certainly not "The Golden State!"

"Gerry ·

Me too! Last week the CA FTB stole almost $2000.00 from my bank account here in Colorado. They took every last penny. I moved out of Southern California in 2006 and did not notify them so according to them they can charge me with not filing a return for 2007 and take my money.

I have faxed them proof I didn't live there but they don't respond and you can't reach them by phone unless you have two hours or more to be put on hold. If someone told me this happened to them before it hit me I would have doubted this is legal. My only hope is the California Taxpayer Ombudsman office. Wish me luck!"

Note: The Taxpayer Ombudsman is a post within the FTB. Getting them on the phone is as difficult as getting the FTB on the line and they will hang up on you, usually while they are talking to make it sound like an accident.

The California Franchise Tax Board has become a rogue bureau and a criminal enterprise, taking money from citizens at will, without regard or legal imperative. In these cases they have both chased people who escaped California or have the same names. Few know how to deal with government ripoffs and are afraid to deal with lawyers

I am sending copies of this to all the leading newspaper Editors, but have little hope of seeing any real action as they are all afraid of government now. They have thrown away what our founders gave them in the Constitution What does it say of American journalism that the likes of a blogger has to break a story of corruption in the California Franchise Tax Board? I expect to obtain more help from the Internet blogging community and perhaps we can embarrass the Governor's office into the action they are required of in the law. The power to tax is the power to destroy."

Donna "

My niece and her husband live in poverty. He is a laborer and she is unemployed. The Franchise tax board attached his wages for a 1992 return he underpaid $153. They claim he now owes $14,500. Even if the interest rate was 100% the absolute most he would owe if interest was compounded monthly is $5000. They went into the FTB office and the clerk gave them a printout saying the balance was $198. Yet she forced them to enter into a payment plan to pay back $14,000 that no one seems to know why they owe.

A few years ago they attached a lien on my Illinois property for taxes they claimed I owed on property that went to my ex husband years before as part of a divorce settlement. I had not lived or worked in CA for more than 10 years. They calculated how much money they felt I earned in CA owed based on the amount of interest my ex paid on a house. Had anyone bothered to check, they would have found recorded documents removing me from the deed and the mortgage.

This is crazy. It is more serious than incompetence. It cost me money to fly to San Diego, obtain the recorded documents and take them to the FTB to remove the lien. My niece and her husband receive food stamps. Yet they have to pay $245 a month or FTB takes what they want out of his check. How can they go back 22 years when we are only required to keep records 7 years. It is an outrage. It absolutely deprives citizens of due process. I think the Attorney General should get involved in this madness.

Note:

For a $153 debt to blow up to $14,000 over 21 years would require a interest rate of 24% compounded, which is illegal in commercial lending, other than credit cards, in every state. Does the FTB issue credit cards. What is it called, "The California Fools Card?" Foolish enough to live in California."

Donna closes with a sentiment we see often in these posts: Many of these people deeply regret they ever lived in California. They feel like they have escaped North Korea. How evil do you have to be do turn "The Golden State" into The People's Republic of California?"

From Anonymous "Is there any way that the Federal government could conduct an investigation of the Franchise Tax Board and all of these various abuses? They did that with the LAPD, the California State Prison, etc. Even the IRS does not stoop to these tactics. Can you bring it to the attention of somebody in the Federal Government? I have dealt with the IRS and they were extremely professional and did not do any of the things that the FTB has done to me. I was able to settle my tax debt with the IRS for pennies on the dollar and I prepared the paperwork myself. The practices of the California Franchise Tax Board need to be brought to the attention of the U.S. Department of Justice, and whatever agency gives them their "franchise."

Note: You must have had a pretty good story or are drop-dead beautiful. I have never been able to squeeze a penny out of those people, but when you have the proof they accept it.

From Amy "

My son, 25, had $852, everything he had in the bank, stolen by the FTB last week on 11/7/13. He owes them nothing. He's filed taxes every year and right now isn't even working as he's a full-time student. He just barely scrapes by. That was his rent money that they stole. He called me in tears after he looked at his balance online. He called the number for FTB the bank gave him and got a recording stating, "Due to large volume of calls, there's a three-hour wait time." This is theft to take someone's money without any warning or ability for the person to explain that this must be a mistake. Shame on them and shame on all DEMOCRATS that have financially driven this state into the ground. If they need money, they should first look to Feinstein and Pelosi, not my kid that's just trying to finish school.

Note: Here again, the FTB violated at least two Constitutions, maybe three, probably made an enemy of a young man forever. They have forever put a crack in the chalice of trust this young man probably had for government. Let us return to the blog entries to view the remains... From Gerry "Hello:

I posted earlier about being ripped off for over $2000.00 by the CA FTB for taxes for the year 2007 when I was not a resident of California and I would just like to say that I still have not heard from the FTB nor the Taxpayers Ombudsman office after numerous faxes and emails. And forget about trying to get through to them by phone. The wait is over two hours now. This is just so crazy but unfortunately it's reality. They really can concoct some flimsy excuse and take all the money they want from you and then you have to desperately fight and fight to get it back.

Gerry"

AV> I responded to this...

Thank you Gerry and I hope to hear from many more and gather enough to get the legislature involved as the FTB's actions violate three Constitutions: The US, California and the state they reach into to take money without notice or court action. In one of these cases they were compounding the late taxes by 24% per year when the CA Constitution limits interest in the state to 7%, which has been amended to 10%, but nothing like 24%. They hanged people in England for that until 1832."

Then we heard from John

"I just received a letter from my bank telling me the FTB was given a $100 processing fee so they can take $1160 from my account in 3 days. Meanwhile, I never lived or worked in California. I worked for a company back in 1999 that was based there but it had an office in Nevada."

<u>AV Response</u>
"I think that was a bank processing fee and when I told Bank of America I would pull all my business if they did not rescind it they complied. Double check your statement and bite back."

From B.E.

"About four months ago, the California FTB took $10,000 from my personal Savings in Texas claiming I mad money in California and I did not declare or pay personal income taxes. I moved out of California in 2005 and have lived and worked only in Texas since then. I had repeatedly received demands from California in 2005 and have lived and worked only in

2005 and have lived and worked only in Texas since then. I had repeatedly received demands from California to pay income tax that I did not owe. I repeatedly responded that I was no longer living or working in California. Still they continued.

Due to the economy, in 2010 I filed for bankruptcy and named the state of California and the FTB just in case they were still to persist. All my debts, including the fraudulently claimed one by the California FTB, were discharged by the bankruptcy court in January 2011. In the early part of this year, I received a demand for payment for income tax for the years 2006 and 2007. They created in income out of thin air in the amount of $250,000 per year and assessed taxes on it! I immediately sent them a response stating and showing that I was not living in California since 2005. All of their correspondence to me and anyone else is to my Texas address and has been all the time. They took the $10,000 from my personal savings after being shown that I was not a resident since 2005 and that any debt to them was discharged in bankruptcy in 2011. Still, they took the money!

I tried to contact them but, after a very long wait, spoke with a number of FTB people who were all trying to make up phony reasons why they were justified. For example, one person said I still have property in California. I responded that I do not. She told which property it was and I told her my interest in that property was quit-claimed to my ex-wife in our divorce in 1995! When I shot down every excuse for their thievery, I was still put off but eventually told to send them proof of everything. Even then, if they agreed to refund my money, they said it will take 90 days to get the check for the refund cut.

They stole my money in a few days. I got a CPA friend of mine in Texas involved in this and she was in contact with the supervisor in charge of my matter. The supervisor admitted to my CPA the FTB staff did not follow regulations nor do the proper checks as they would have seen the property was not mine since 1995. The supervisor then told my CPA they would cut a check that day and mail it to me. That was almost three months ago and now my CPA is being put off when she tries to call to find out what is going on.

Undoubtedly, everything the FTB does is fraudulent, theft, and complete lies. The kicker in all this? I asked them if they had a right to take a disabled veteran's benefit payments. I was told "No." I asked if they can take child support payments. I was told "No." I asked if they can take monies received from an annuity created to pay for injuries due to being hit by a drunk driver. I was told "No." I told them the funds they took from that bank account are all from those three sources. The responded "Can you prove it is 100% from those sources?" I said yes. Still they wanted to dispute that I could not have that amount of money from those sources.

I am a disabled Vietnam vet (served in the Marine Corps 1964 to 1968. Was in Vietnam 1966-67) who is constantly being treated. I receive compensation from the VA for my injuries. I am a divorced single parent who receives child support . I was hit head-on by a drunk driver (he was killed and I suffered, and continue to suffer, problems from that accident) on the freeway in 1985 and receive a monthly annuity. The money in the savings account is from these sources and I was saving everything so my child can go to the college of her choice. The FTB took it without any legal right whatsoever and is lying about paying it back. If the average person did this, the Attorney General would have filed criminal charges against him/her and jailed that person. If it was corporate criminality, the executives and managers of the company would have been put on criminal trial and the company shut down.

Since these are state employees and protected by law for their malfeasance, their outright thievery and fraudulently created lies and excuses to justify their actions, we have a tremendously difficult time getting their intentional theft corrected. I loved California for many years. There is no wonder it has become what it is now. Incompetent state employees and out-and-out thieves hired by the state have dragged it into being the economic cesspool it is. Everyone who lives in, or has lived in, California should be very wary and protect them-selves with a huge paper trail. Even then it will be a long and idiotic fight with state officials who refuse to acknowledge the truth as it will show their incompetence, negligence and criminal behavior. For all these years, I had bragged about how nice California is. Now, I cannot say anything. The geography is wonderful. The California state officials are turning the state into a hell hole."

Note: When I read this story I thought I had seen it all, but this is not the only one of this kind, to this depth, with this much pain and disbelief it engenders on reading or hearing. How much humanity does it take to want to find the truth? That is what is most shocking about these stories. To think that the state of California tolerates this from government employees is shocking, but to realize they encourage it is only to lose faith in your fellow man."

From Jesus "Hi I'm devastated I don't know what to do the FTB debited my account for more than $17 thousand. They wouldn't give me much information when I called. I moved out of the state of California in 1998 and sold my property I filed taxes and they are claiming I owe the state of California money for not telling them that I had moved out! I currently live in Texas I file taxes and the small amount of money I did have I was planning to use for my retirement. What can I do since I live in Texas and the bank is not willing to help me?"

Note: Here is a man alone, apparently not well

educated in the ways of an evil government taking every advantage of him and what to do about it. How can they be surprised when someone shows up with an AK 47 and sweeps the first floor with bullets? Government people like these cause revolutions.

Anonymous" wrote:
"Two months ago, while I was unemployed and receiving unemployment payments from the State of California EDD, the FTB seized my checking account without notice, taking everything in it. I called the FTB collections immediately the next morning and they said I had underpaid taxes for five random past years going back as far as 2001 and they had filed a "Noce of Lien" against me for over $6000. (During any one of those years I would not have owed the FTB any more than $300 at the most. Having said that, I am due a refund of over $1,000 for 2011 and 2012 (each), which they will not send me because they said it was applied to my outstanding tax debt!

They owe me money. However, they claim that I somehow owe them $6,000 in taxes, penalties and interest since 2001. Three weeks ago, after being unemployed for three months I finally began a temp job. Last Friday I received a copy of an Order to garnish my wages 25%. I called the FTB again and explained to them that they owe me money for 2011 and 2012 refunds, but again I have been told that this is being applied to the $6,000 debt.

"We get paid first" were the FTB agent's exact words. I explained that taking 25% of my wages was a hardship. To boot, I am one of the 20,000 Californians who never received my last unemployment check, which was due to me for the two-week period ending September 9, 2013, That is $900. I told the collections agent this: "I did not get my last unemployment check and I am behind financially already in basic needs." Her response was "Everybody knows people didn't get their unemployment check! That's been on the news!" The only way she would release the Order to garnish my wages was if I agreed to have $45 per week taken out of my temp job pay, so I agreed.

It is obvious to me that the FTB has hired private collection agents to do their bidding and to collect money from anybody and everybody right now. I believe it is illegal, since there was no due process, and I doubt the Notice of Lien is an actual legal lien.

There is a 4 year statue of limitation on debt collection. If I owed FTB for an underpayment in 2001, I should have been notified much, much sooner. They are using any discrepancy they can find in anybody's taxes, going as far back as they want to, and then adding outrageous penalties and interest completely out of balance with the minimal tax amounts that might be due. Even the IRS informs you of your rights to settle for pennies on the dollar through the Offer in Compromise. These collection agents who are filing these erstwhile "Notices of Lien" and seizing bank accounts, garnishing wages, keeping tax refunds are not skilled tax board employees. They are junkyard dog collection agents."

Note: This is a most impressive, lucid, well-informed and legally aware response in this set. This man or woman is just the kind who would make an excellent witness for the plaintiff at a trial of the FTB Gestapo. We have another "Anonymous," who writes:

"If you are experiencing a similar problem, the only tips I can give are: do not keep money in your bank account; call the FTB as soon as they open in the morning (7:30 am) and demand written proof of the debt; ask them to snail-mail you a complete assessment that you "owe", including all penalties and interest; ask them to send you an "economic hardship form". (I was told that if my temp job ends I can file an "economic hardship" form of some kind with them to temporarily halt collection.

If they are garnishing your wages, tell them that you can pay a small amount on an installment plan, but try to do this without it being done through your employer. I am not sure how I will be able to get my employer to stop withholding the $45 each week! They have to comply with the Order."

Note: All good tactics, but isn't it heartbreaking to think America has come to this?

From B.E.
"Did I hear "class action suit in federal court?" It is about time and there are many plaintiffs nationwide. It may very well be possible. Federal court will probably give all affected a fairer shake whereas a California judge just might be worried about his/her job should we prevail. Any suggestions from anyone?"

B.E. writes back:

"Please see my comment regarding a class action suit? We should, where possible, name the FTB, the State of California, all the FTB officials, the Governor, the California politicians who have the responsibility to oversee the financial and taxing agencies of California, etc. A monumental task but one that is necessary to achieve fairness in California. They have rigged the game by setting the rules and still they do not follow them. That is fraud and thievery. Anyone else would be in prison by now.
http://www.yelp.com/biz/state-of-california-franc... I don't even LIVE in California. I have never

Note: "B.E." makes a good point: This class action will have to be filed in the Federal courts as it involves more than one state and there is no doubt

that a California judge would think twice about
finding against the FTB.

Kate H writes:

"Sign me up !!! And if you go to this YELP page..
there is a ton of complains there too !
been farther west than Alabama and they locked up
my joint account I have with my husband - who has
also never lived in California !!!   W.T.F. !!!"

Note: The link no longer works, but this is the most
important aspect of this case: The California
Franchise Tax board is picking people literally "out
of the blue," and taking millions of Dollars from
them with the aid of banks! Banks that are so eager
to collect high "legal transaction" fees they will
commit felonies! Now tell me how far we have
fallen. And, what do we have to do to get back?"
Note: Bernie Madow showed how long a man can
stay out of jail if he has held a high position and has
highly placed friends. Corruption is our biggest
problem. It has destroyed every great empire from
within. Nonetheless, if we can impress the Governor
that we are serious and have the goods we will soon
see him on our side as "survival" is the first instinct
of politicians."

Casey commented:

"I would have love to make a huge publicity to expose the massive corruption process California has been following. Whatever they are doing is totally unfair and as a citizen of California everyone deserves a notice or apology for what they're doing constantly."

Note: Lefties love to apologize for some deeply psychological reason normal people cannot understand, but "lefties" get off on it. The kicker is that they never suffer any consequences and if you ask them about it they say, "Well, I apologized! I took responsibility! What difference does it make?"

Again "B.E." comments:

"Another wrinkle in my quest for justice: As I posted before, the overseeing FTB supervisor said they did not follow procedure and unjustifiably took my money from my bank account. He also said they would cut a check for the amount and send it back to me that day. That was two months ago. Today, I found out from my bank they have attached $4,000 more! The FTB and its personnel lie. I am going to file suit this week."

Note: I hope "B.E." has a lot of money as the FTB has a whole department of attorneys, one of whom told me the statute of limitations "does not matter, what difference does it make?" and this was a lady who sounded very much like Hillary Clinton. In an honest state with an honest bar association that lady

would lose her license to practice law forever.
Solo Ed wrote:

"My heart goes out to all who have been victimized by the California FTB. They stole from me also last year. I did my taxes on Turbo-tax, calculated everything perfectly, re-checked all the numbers, and then filed. U.S. Treasury gave me my return in 3 weeks. California sent me $125.00 less than my refund should have been. They sent me a letter stating "Your refund was adjusted downward for the following reason: SEE CODE(s) BELOW:

When I read the code attached to my case, it stated "Refund based on maximum allowable deductions". What the hell does that mean? It means nothing of course, they just wanted my money; more money. They said I could challenge this by sending a letter of appeal. They listed an address in Sacramento. I sent the letter and never heard back. The State is just stealing money from its residents. They are rogue and must be stopped."

Note: We certainly agree. The California Franchise Tax Board has become a criminal enterprise under Democrat control.

Kate H:

"I came across this post by doing a search on complaints about the California FTB. My husband and I just had our bank account frozen because of these a-shats.

We live in GEORGIA and have NEVER lived, worked or even visited California. So I have no idea what gave them the right to take our funds. The GOOD news is that we only had $76 in our accounts total, but what sucks is its our joint account and now its locked up. How the hell are we supposed to pay our bills? Or feed our children? Or pay for gas to get to/from work after my paycheck hits Friday night?!?!! Someone PLEASE tell me there is something we can do !!!!!"

Note: When we Googled "Complaints about the California Franchise Tax Board" we got 6,220,000 hits! Out of curiosity I did the same search on BING and got 18,800.000! Three times more on Bing than Google. Why?

B_Dobbs:

"The state of California has just frozen my bank account. They claim I owe over $39,000 from 02, 03, 04. I was born and raised in the state but left in 2001 and never returned. They claim I held a license in the state for those years, and since I never filed they assume that I could have earned 79k per year. This is ridiculous. I only used the license for a few months in

98, and it has been expired since 2000. This has got to be criminal. How can this be allowed?"

Note: So if you get a professional license in California you owe them 10% of your income, or what they think your income should be, in perpetuity. When will the California Franchise Tax Board start attending funerals and handing big bills to widows?"

Anonymous:"

Ask your bank for the phone number at the FTB to call; your bank will have been given the number. Call them ASAP and tell them this (that you never earned any money as a licensed professional after1998 and that license has been expired since 2000.) Ask them to SEND YOUR EVIDENCE of any earnings in California for those years. Tell them to rebate whatever money they took out of your account back to your account.

If they tell you to file tax returns for those years, ask for the forms to be sent to you along with their proof of your earnings in California for those years. And if you had no earnings for those years, tell them that you have zero earnings to report, or only have other earnings, not from that licensed profession. In other words, they have to send you proof of earnings. You have the right to file a zero-income tax return. Also, contact the IRS and get your Adjusted Gross Income for the years in question. You will need that information to file your California tax returns (assuming that your income was earned in California.)

I am not a tax professional by any means, but I had my account seized for underpaying, and I asked them to send me my earnings for those years since I no longer had that information. The problem is, I still needed my Adjusted Gross Income from my federal returns, because it is lower than the amount the FTB gives you. I hope this helps. They do have the ability to just reverse the money back into your account, but you need to call them and contest it and also follow up in writing, document what they tell you in the phone call and what you tell them."

Note: This sounds good, but it is predicated on the assumption you are dealing with honest people and there is more than abundant evidence that we are not. The more important point that Anonymous makes is that if you make an intelligent, powerful response, as it is hoped this work will prepare you to do, you have a chance of prevailing. This tells me that at some level the FTB knows they could have a come-uppance, someone could prevail over them in a way that could hurt and it is our objective here to find it.

This begs the question: "When will Governor Brown put a stop to this?" He is totally responsible according to the California Attorney General and we suspect it is he could suffer most if this story breaks.

A. McGill" commented:"Yes, it is true if you have a license, the taxing "authorities" seem to think you have made the money. This happened to me when I had a license to sell Insurance. I made NO sales but was dunned for the taxes that a typical Insurance salesperson would have made. Do these people just make it up as they go along? Whatever happened to the "Rule of Law?" Whatever happened to honesty? Yes, the IRS, FTB and all other taxing agencies have to pay for all the fat salaries, fat healthcare and fat pensions, somehow."

Note: You left out bonuses, A. McGill. The Federal and state bureaus now pay large performance bonuses at the end of every year, in some cases equal to the annual salary. The more they recover, the more the bonus. Plus, more and more Federal and state bureau employees are not paying their taxes, and nothing happens to them! The entire system has become totally corrupt.

"mike" commented…

"Yep, the CA FTB is something else. An Illinois company made an investment in a Delaware LLC. The CA FTB is dunning the IL business over $3,000 for franchise taxes from 2010 based on the assumption they are 'doing business in California.

The IL company owns .0003% of the LLC and the share of CA income? $0.00 - nothing. But CA is threatening to file a lien and a lawsuit to recover money they're not entitled to. What a ripoff!!"
Note: This again brings up the "collecting taxes across state lines" issue which is utterly unconstitutional and this is where the FTB is way-out-of -line.

@day22white: "A lot of the FTB people think they can write up any purely speculative nonsense as a reason for a tax. They seem to do this often. It is probably not illegal for them to do this. However, even if you do not answer in time. They are committing a crime as soon as they attach any of your money on a false excuse."

Note: While "@dav22white" hit on the mind of the FTB bureau, we could not object more strongly If they can imagine the income you owe them then our reality becomes whatever a Washington or Sacramento bureaucrat thinks it to be. That is the mind of a Nazi Gestapo.
@dav22white continued...

"They can claim you didn't respond (or didn't respond in the way they wanted); but if their excuse for taking your money is false, their actions are criminal. They cannot (as some of them seem to think they can) make up any BS they want. Then bill you and take your money if you do not pay the bill.

They do have the power to take your money; but they do not have the right. They are criminal if they take it based on a false premise. I tend to think the threatening messages they sometimes send also amount to extortion. The law is probably murky if you give in; and you send them what they ask for. However, if you do not, they are criminal if they take it. Writing up some BS does not qualify in law as proof that you owe them money."

Note: They only have the "power" when the banks cooperate with them, and they do because they make outrageous fees for nothing. You cannot trust your banker. It is cause to leave your bank after they have executed such a transaction and we think a cause of action in the Court of Small Claims where you prosecute your own case and we say win.

@dav22white wrote: "If you think about it, the FTB threatening to attach all of your assets when you really owe them nothing, is the same as hoodlum demanding money from a business in order to not destroy it; extortion. If they are threatening to attach all of your assets, which is their typical behavior for going after a debt, they are within their rights if you actually owe it. If you don't owe it, they are extorting money from you. In law if you do not owe anything, they cannot by any deadline scheme they use cause you to owe them. If they manufacture a debt out of thin air, they are guilty of fraud as soon as they threaten to attach your assets for not paying their manufactured debt.

They are probably more guilty in law if they actually attach your assets. From what I am reading on the internet recently, someone needs to file RICO charges against them. Jerry Brown is encouraging them to be aggressive. Some employees are ignoring the rule of law in their pursuit of this aggression. I am convinced they are also after bonuses and raises. This makes their crime more serious. Jerry Brown has to know this kind of thing is going on, yet he is not moving to stop it. That makes him complicit. Ditto the head of the FTB. Note: "@dav22white" is dead on right. When I talked with the Attorney General she told me that per law she was assigned to protect the FTB from people like me! When I asked who had oversight she said, "Governor Brown!" Talk about the fox in the chicken coop! Here is the guy most desperate for money and is he going to tell his primary collectors to slow down when he is $100 billion in the hole? As Rush Limbaugh says, "Follow the money!"

Miffed:

"I received a letter from FTB stating I owe taxes. I had my taxes offset in 98-99-2K and 2k1 for five thousand Dollars in student loans, for an LVN Licensed Vocational Nurse program. The offsets totaled over 12K which should have been more than enough to pay off the $5,000 in student loans plus interest I received.

I Left California in 2002 had no income to report as I didn't work. We were stationed in AZ in 2002 and I have not had any income in this state or any other state since. I'm a stay-at-home mom. I called and was placed on hold for 2.5 hours only to finally connect with someone that hung up. I don't owe any taxes. I have nothing to levy. I will be looking into class actions." Note: "Miffed" can only hope that we find a legal foundation to take this on and she would certainly be welcome to the class. The two-and-one-half hour wait is usual and probably contrived, meaning they make you wait that longer whether or not they are busy. TyraT: "FTB placed a levy on my bank accounts. I did not receive any type of notification. I have been at the same job for three years and the same home address for two. This is just ridiculous, they did not give me a chance to petition the levy or anything, I am not sure what the debt is for. On top of that today is a holiday therefore I had to go all weekend with my children plus today without access to any of my money.

Note: This is clearly illegal. We assume TyraT is a California resident, which already makes her a second class citizen as they are now giving license to practice law to people who commit felonies by being here without documentation so stealing money from citizens fits them like a condom.

"Adam"

"I grew up in California but moved to DC in 2004 at the age of 17. I have not lived in CA since then. In 2009 I accidentally wrote down my parents CA address when filing taxes. In 2013 my parents received a notice that I owed the state taxes for 2009. I immediately called in and was told that all I needed to do was fax a copy of my w-2 for 2009 which I did. I was told that this would suffice. Fast forward to November 2013, when I went to deposit funds in my bank account, all my funds were gone because of an LL1 order from the CA Franchise Tax Board. I called and again was told I would need to submit the W-2 again. I did, and was told my account would be released immediately.

I also told them that my bank was charging $125 legal processing fee and that I would need a statement of error from them to have that removed. They say that since I had written the wrong address that there was no error on their part. This, even though they didn't communicate through mail as they had both my current DC address and parent's permanent address,

Fast forward to the day after they were supposed to have released my accounts. I had to wait two hours to get through to the office, and they told me they still hadn't released because of an office error. Is it me or am I paying for some idiots in an office to not do their jobs? They also refused to send a letter of error, leaving me out $125, and now I have to go to my bank and negotiate the overdraft fees I incurred from having my student loan payments go through automatically on the same day they took all my funds.

What can I do? I am infuriated. I am someone that is very responsible and believes in paying on time and being on top of my finances, but when someone else messes up, why am I being penalized?"

Note: Adam: Call or go to the bank and get ask for a manager or someone in authority. Explain the problem to him, step-by-step, as you have done here and finish that saying, "If I cannot obtain 100% recovery I will take my account to another bank and I will badmouth this bank for the rest of my life, and then put your hand down as if you were making a solemn pledge. I guarantee you, they will comply.

Marie: "I did not file federal taxes one year and they have been trying to get money from me also. My strategy when I moved out of that thieving state was opening an account in another state's bank that has no branches in California. So far my money seems safe. I too would join in a class action suit to have their unfounded lien showing up on my credit report wiped out. Sorry you all are going through this. I've been waiting for the day enough are impacted so FTB overreaching can be challenged on a federal level."

Note: Only doing business in state charted banks is a very good idea for many reasons. The Federal government is now entertaining the idea of seizing funds as they have seen several European countries do it with very little citizen protest! That would not be the case in America. We are truly exceptional.

Janet:

"I was not a resident of California when in 2006 my mother passed away and I inherited part of my mother's house. Some capital gains accrued and I did not realize this. The trustee withheld the proper amount of taxes but out of misunderstanding I did not file a tax return.

Since I live in the Netherlands, I never heard a word from the FTB. Then a few months ago I received a letter from my USA bank stating that the FTB had cleaned the account out due to unpaid taxes. I hope that they will allow me to pay just the penalty for not filing. That I can accept but not multiple years of interest against a tax bill that was incorrect in the first place.
You really have to be careful with any dealings with the state of California. It seems as if they use any excuse to tax people with even the most slight association to the place.

Note: Janet while you may be innocent in your heart you are guilty as sin in the eyes of the law. They will give you no respite in this matter. As they say "Ignorance of the law is no excuse," but they passed 40,000 new laws in the US every year now and do not expect lawyers to know all of them to the point of requiring them to specialize. I doubt you will get any sympathy from the Franchise Tax Board, but the IRS is a different matter. I have been audited many times having had multiple sources of income, and some foreign, two corporations and other complications. On two occasions I made mistakes and the IRS only want the appropriate tax to be paid. Of them I cannot complain. Next we have a comment by:

Outraged Floridian

"Wow I cannot believe how many people are getting this. I too have received a letter from them. I have never lived in California, never worked there either and have done no business in California. What is going on here?"

Note: Sir we would all like an answer to that question and get our money back to too! The next to comment was by:

Barbara:

"The Franchise Tax Board just stole nearly $700 from me. Months ago I received notice that I owed them over $9,000 for the tax year 2011. Interesting, since I was a student and had no income in 2011. So I called them and they told me they estimated that I owed that amount based on the average salary for someone with my professional law license in 2011. So I politely informed them that I did not obtain said professional license until December 2011, a fact easily verified on the public California Bar website, and furthermore was not employed until 2012. Everything resolved, right?

Nope, last month I saw a chunk of my paycheck deducted. I called the bank and was informed my wages were garnished by the Franchise Tax Board. I called them and got the same spiel after waiting on hold for three hours. The lady I talked to either doesn't understand English or lacks the intellectual capacity to understand that I cannot be presumed to make the average salary for a license before I have the license. She admitted she had no evidence that I had income in 2011.

Whose burden is it to prove my income? Mine? I had to provide her with school transcripts and loan statements before she would stop the garnishment. So I demanded to talk to someone else and was informed there is no one else to talk to. I asked for a hearing before a judge and was told I have no right to one. She then, oh so graciously, agreed to abate the garnishment for a month so I can provide her with proof of my lack of income.

Ridiculous. Where is due process? Under what authority can the government take my money based on speculation-even after I have demonstrated this speculation is false?"

AV> You are right and they are wrong. If you live within 150 miles of the Franchise Tax Board you can sue them in your County Court of Small Claims that handle cases with damages up to $10,000, maybe more. The filing fee is $14 and the service by registered mail is a few Dollars. In a month you will go to trial and they will have to send someone to defend the FTB or lose by default. Attorneys are not allowed in the Court of Small Claims as representatives, but you are the plaintiff and you should be able to nail them to the door. If they cannot produce evidence the judge will decide for you and you may ask for and get assumed damages for your suffering over this matter. Be sure to ask the judge to "test the defendant" which means they have to give you a bank account and number so you can collect the money, plus court costs and collection charges.

Guest 123

"One of my family members just became a victim. Before my father passed away, he asked me to be the administrator for a college education fund he set up for my niece. I was living in CA at that time - My niece, my father, and all my other relatives lived on the east coast. My niece was nine years old at the time."

I did the federal/ IRS taxes and the MARYLAND taxes for my niece. None of this had anything whatsoever to do with California. Somehow they must have ILLICITLY got her IRS info - I left California in 2003 –

And recently, they sent her a letter saying she owed CA taxes plus interest and penalties for tax year 2003. She replied to them that she has NEVER, EVER lived in CA or derived any income from a CA business, and doesn't owe them any money!

Without any further notice or due process, they removed all the money from her checking account. This is an outrage!"

Note: I certainly agree that this is an outrage and I am amazed that so many banks will cooperate with the California Franchise Tax Board to take money from their clients when they are legally obligated to protect their money. The banks would be held liable in a court case.

I think we who have been harmed by these banks have a cause of action as a class. There is a lot of money in this for the people the California Franchise Tax Board has attacked with the help of the banks.

Next we hear from: Kristen "My husband and I have been fighting the California Franchise Tax Board for years. We previously lived in California, and now live in Oregon. The CA FTB continues to levy our bank accounts with no notice. I hired a lawyer at a considerable cost to fight them, they continued to insist his office did not send the documents the CA FTB required, even though they were sent certified with signature required. We have proof that they received the documents. Four years later I am still fighting them. They are still cleaning out our bank accounts on a regular basis, and continue to claim that we owe them money we do not owe. When they ignore lawyers, what are we supposed to do? How do we get these criminals to stop harassing us and stealing our money?"

Note: It would certainly seem you have a cause of action against the bank and why your attorney is not acting puts him in question too. Unfortunately, when a bureau denies getting legal papers they can get away with it as no one is keeping oversight on them. Governor Brown clearly endorses every Dollar they glean. California is clearly, and totally, corrupt when they give an illegal alien a license to practice law. Next we hear from:

Helpfulhints:

"Direct access to FTB 916-845-7319. My bank gave me this number. They answer every single time."

AV> Thank you and that is a good number to have, And now we hear from:

Luann: "How do we start a class action lawsuit against these criminals at the FTB? They do whatever they want and do not follow the law. I say we charge them as the criminals they are. We all need to put liens on their surety bonds." Note: We need to find a very rich lawyer or conservative legal action organization, and I will be getting in touch with several. They need to define a class, which means getting a lot of victims to sign on. We may be able to subpoena a list of victims, but they will never give us a complete list. We can only hope many will come forward. Next we hear from:

Gerry Lavelle

"There is a ray of light available in the darkness of being victimized by these crooks: The CA FTB stole all the money from my bank accounts at the end of June 2013 and to compound the misery from this event my bank waited six days to notify me of this situation thus letting me run up expensive overdraft fees. As soon as I was notified of the seizure of my funds I knew it was the CA FTB even though the bank would not tell me who seized the funds. I had already had a run-in with the CA FTB back in 2008 because of supposedly owing taxes for 2007 even though I had moved from California in 2006. This matter had supposedly been settled after I faxed the CA FTB extensive documented proof that I didn't reside in California in 2007 nor any time since.

Five years later they seized all my funds and cost me expensive overdraft fees. They are basically unreachable by phone, email or fax. Luckily, I learned about the CA Taxpayers Advocates Office so I contacted them and they stepped in, straightened the mess out and I got my money back. They are basically the good guys in comparison to the CA FTB's bad guys. They are reachable by phone after just 15-20 minutes on hold instead of hours and hours like CA FTB. They listen to your story and take action on it. They even followed up on CA FTB saying that my case was being resolved and then once again losing the paperwork so that there was no record of me in their system.

The Advocates Office got them to fast track my case and I got my money back pronto! However, the last screwed-up thing the CA FTB did to me was to give my money back in form of a refund they reported to the IRS as if I were getting a tax refund owed when it was money they had stolen from my bank account.

And finally, if I want the money back from all the overdraft fees I have to sue the CA FTB and it's my word against theirs about whether or not they knew in 2008 that I documented proof of non-residency. Since they claim to have lost all that paperwork there is no proof that I had settled the case with them. So I will take the victory of getting most of my money back and let it go."

Note: While going after them for full compensation may seem futile I am sorry you are not doing it as that is the only way we the people have of putting a stop to this, i.e. take the profit out of it. I believe many people pay the duns rather than fight it out of fear for the worst and as they say, "You can't fight city hall," but we have to. Not fighting them makes them more arrogant and evil. Let's see what happened to:

Michelle "I just checked my bank account today (4 days before Christmas) and saw there was a POS Transaction for $707 and another $100 fee. Called my bank and they told me that there was a transaction pending from the California Franchise Tax Board and a processing fee. We used to live in California but have lived in Washington State for five years now. I don't know what this is for and I had no warning. This transaction showed up on my account on a Saturday. My bank gave me an account number for the transaction and a phone number. I called and of course it was closed but it gave me a link. I went to the link and put the account number and my last name but there is no record of those matching. Does anyone have any information on this matter?"

Note: Michelle, you will have to call them as they do not answer letters; just take more money. So far the best suggestion we have heard is that of calling the California Taxpayers Advocates Office and their number is 800-883-5910, FAX 916-855-2101 They are within the FTB but many have reported getting good results from them.

Note: And something from the:business, franchise & investment expo by a man named Adam: "I grew up in California but moved to DC in 2004 at the age of 17. I have not lived in CA since then. In 2009 I accidentally wrote down my parents CA address when filing taxes. In 2013 my parents received a notice that I owed the state taxes for 2009. I immediately called in and was told that all I needed to do was fax a copy of my w-2 for 2009 which I did. I was told that this would suffice.

Fast forward to November 2013, when I went to deposit funds into my bank account, all my funds were gone because of an LL1 order from the CA tax board. I called in and again was told I would need to submit the W2 again. I do, and am told that my account will be released immediately.

I also told them my bank was charging $125 legal processing fee and I would need a statement of error from them to have removed. They say that since I had written the wrong address there was no error on their part. This, even though they didn't communicate through mail (they had both my current DC address and parent's permanent address), or through phone(they had my cell phone).

Fast forward to the day after they were supposed to have released my accounts. I had to wait two hours to get through to the office, and they told me they still haven't released because of an office error. Is it me or am I paying for some idiots in an office to not do their jobs? They also refused to send a letter of error, leaving me out $125, and now I have to go to my bank and negotiate all the overdraft fees I incurred from having my student loan payments go through automatically (on the same day they took all my funds).

What can I do? I am infuriated. I am someone that is very responsible and believes in paying on time and being on top of my finances, but when someone else messes up, why am I being penalized?"

Note: What the FTB has done is illegal. This is the nature of government. There are things you can do without having to spend a lot of money, as we outline here, but it will take some time. Next, we heard from: Marie: I did not file federal taxes one year and they have been trying to get money from me also. My strategy when I moved out of that thieving state was opening an account in another state's bank that has no branches in California. So far my money seems safe. I too would join in a class action suit to have their unfounded lien showing up on my credit report wiped out. Sorry you all are going through this. I've been waiting for the day enough are impacted so FTB overreaching can be challenged on a federal level."

Note: I am hoping we can make that day come. So far they have gotten away with grand theft on a major scale. We move on to the comment by:

Guest 123 One of my family members just became a victim. Before my father passed, he asked me to be the administrator for a college education fund he set up for my niece [his granddaughter]

I was living in CA at that time - My niece, my father, and all my other relatives lived on the east coast. My niece was 9 years old at the time.

I did the federal/ IRS taxes and the MARYLAND taxes for my niece - none of this had anything whatsoever to do with California at all! Somehow they must have ILLICITLY got her IRS information. I left California in 2003.

And recently, they sent her a letter saying she owed CA taxes plus interest and penalties for tax year 2003.She replied to them that she has NEVER, EVER lived in CA or derived any income from a CA business, and doesn't owe them any money! Now, without any further notice or due process at all, they just removed all the money from her checking account! This is an outrage!

Please everyone, we need to make this info of this lawless criminal activity by California GO VIRAL!!

Please send this information with Stephen Frank's link - http://capoliticalnews.com/2013/08/18/adrian-vance... to all your favorite news media - especially the ALTERNATIVE MEDIA - and to political blogs, political meet-up groups, etc!

Please send to any and all political media - left wing, right wing, and center! We want EVERYBODY to know about this travesty! If you are a victim, you can also inform your own Senators and Congressional Rep, as well as your state Senators and Assembly Rep. and we also need to find one or more strong groups to help us remedy this - possibly a non-profit justice oriented law group."

Note: This is much more than a comment; it is a plan for action. This is an issue ripe for action by an existing action group or a new one forming.

Kristen writes:

"My husband and I have been fighting the California Franchise Tax Board for years. We previously lived in California, and now live in Oregon. The CA FTB continues to levy our bank accounts with no notice. I hired a lawyer at a considerable cost to fight them, they continued to insist his office did not send the documents the CA FTB required, even though they were sent certified with signature required. We have proof that they received the documents. Four years later I am still fighting them. They are still cleaning out our bank accounts on a regular basis, and continue to claim that we owe them money we do not owe. When they ignore lawyers, what are we supposed to do? How do we get these criminals to stop harassing us and stealing our money?

Helpfulhint:

"Direct access to FTB 916-845-7319. My bank gave me this number. They answer every single time." Next... Luann writes: How do we start a class action lawsuit/victim report against these criminal at the FTB? they do whatever they want and do not follow the law......I say we charge them as the criminal they are....we all need to put liens on their surety bonds." Note: We want to find a conservative organization that is interested in biting into an issue where we can win and make a real difference in the economy of California and America. Gerry Lavelle "There is a ray of light available in the darkness of being victimized by these crooks: The CA FTB stole all the money from my bank accounts at the end of June 2013 and to compound the misery from this event my bank waited six days to notify me of this situation thus letting me run up expensive overdraft fees. As soon as I was notified of the seizure of my funds I knew it was the CA FTB even though the bank would not tell me who seized the funds. I had already had a run-in with the CA FTB back in 2008 because of supposedly owing taxes for 2007 even though I had moved from California in 2006. This matter had supposedly been settled after I faxed the CA FTB extensive documented proof that I didn't reside in California in 2007 nor any time since.

Now five years later they seized all my funds and cost me expensive overdraft fees. They are basically unreachable by phone, email or fax. Luckily, I learned about the CA Taxpayers Advocates Office so I contacted them and they stepped in and straightened the mess out and I got my money back. They are basically the good guys in comparison to the CA FTB's bad guys. They are reachable by phone after just 15-20 minutes on hold instead of hours and hours like CA FTB. They listen to your story and take action on it. They even followed up on CA FTB saying that my case was being resolved and then once again losing the paperwork so that there was no record of me in their system.

The Advocate Office got them to fast track my case and I got my money back -- pronto! However, the last screwed-up thing the CA FTB did to me was to give my money back in form of a refund that was reported to the IRS like I was getting refund on taxes owed when it was money they basically stole from my bank account because their own incompetence or malicious greed. And finally, if I want the money back from all the overdraft fees I have to sue the CA FTB and it's my word against theirs about whether or not they knew in 2008 that I documented proof of non-residency. Since they lost all that paperwork there is no proof that I had supposedly settled the case with them. So I will take the victory of getting most of my money back and let it go."

Note:

"...the bank would not tell me who seized the funds." What? This is a bank that should be put out of business on that fact alone. They have violated the Constitutions of two states and the United States. Gerry should get much more than her money. Michelle

"I just checked my bank account today (4 days before Christmas) and saw there was a POS Transaction for $707 and another $100 fee. Called my bank and they told me that there was a transaction pending from the California Franchise Tax Board and a processing fee. We used to live in California but have lived in Washington State for 5 years now. I don't know what this is for but I had no warning. This transaction showed up on my account on a Saturday. My bank gave me an account number for the transaction and a phone number. I called and of course its closed but it gave me a link. I went to the link and put the account number and my last name but there is no record of those matching. Does anyone have any information on this matter?"

Note: The best people to call are the California FTB Taxpayer Advocates Office at 800 883 5910 and you can FAX them letters and documents at 916-855-5910. The FAX does not give you a callback confirmation so save whatever documentation your FAX produces.

In spite of that office being part of the FTB they are well known for doing very good, honest work. I have a feeling they are there to keep the FTB from stepping on the feet of people who will kick back and perhaps produce documents, like a book, that could get them in real trouble. If that is true, then we are dealing with a very sophisticated scam.

Christian Manceras

"I too just became a victim of this FTB.. I have not lived nor worked in California since 2008. And now they put a block on my account.. And now my payroll check is in limbo because of this... I previously contacted them because they were trying to get me for taxes during my overseas duty in Japan.

Stating that I owe taxes because I lived there.. I called them up and spoke with a representative and told them I wasn't living in California and provided information of my address and proof of this and the representative stated it's our mistake and we will wipe this clean from your record.

After that I thought it was resolved, but I guess not.. I was never given notice about this and had to find out by my bank stating they put a freeze on just account.. I mean do they have such power to do such a thing to people... Putting people into more of a bind so they are unable to get the basic needs to live.. Since they froze my account I have getting overdraft fees and can't make a deposit.. I am currently in Saudi Arabia working for a Saudi company.. Anyone know who I can contact so that I can get this resolved as quickly as possible? I need help urgently... Thanks everyone.. And if anyone is filing a class suit I would like to be part of it.. This branch of government has gone too far and has made so much peoples lives miserable because of it."

Note: This is very consistent with many other stories of the FTB: You will seem to get a resolution, a clerk will tell you all is well with your documents and the matter is resolved. Six months later you get another bill or they raid your bank account! They are doing this in a way where they can claim that it was a bureaucratic error, but it seems likely that they are hoping to wear you out to the point you will not resist, but let them take your money. This, if true, makes them utterly evil."

Miss Dee writes: "In 2002 I left CA. I did not file taxes because I receive social security disability, therefore not required to do so. I receive care from my daughter who lives in CA and my parents in Florida. Over the past year and a half have spent approximately 5 months in CA. In 2007 while living in NYC they sent me a letter stating I owed them back taxes for 2002. I called & explained I did not owe and only received $7,400 that year in disability payments. They asked me for a letter of proof from social security and told me they would review again. If they find I still owe them they will have me fill out a hardship form which should get approved based on my proof of limited income. I did not hear back from them until I received a letter last May 2013. Now they say I owe them back taxes of almost $28,000. Again I called them and was asked for a letter from social security. I complied and did not receive anything from them since. No letters, no phone calls.

However, on December 18th I received a letter from Bank of America stating the FTB has and will take all my fun only for the next ten business days and that they've assessed a $150 per transaction fee. So for two cents literally that I had in my savings account , the other thief Bank of America is charging me.

What part of the Social Security Act 207 do they both not understand:. I am 100% disabled with a life threatening disease. I struggle each and every month of my life and TONIGHT they will illegally steal my money, rape me of any possibility of survival, starve me and drive me of my medication which will cause me a set back in my life.   This is America. The Franchise Tax Board of California needs to be stopped. Their employees need to be trained to follow the law and that it is not their job to destroy lives. In ten days the FTB has destroyed my life. By January 10th, my 2 dogs and I will be thrown out of my rented apartment. By January 10th I will be sick because I will not have my needed medication, by January 10th I will be famished because I cannot afford food or gas. By January 15th I will plea to the Lord to take me because the FTB will continue to torture me till death. Leave me alone and put your efforts where the real monies owed can be collected. Leave all of us challenged individuals to live the best way we can with limitations."

Note: What more need we see to appreciate the imperative there is on this issue: To go through this bureau with the scythe of the law, justice and the punishments these people richly deserve.

Guest 123:

"Freedom Law School beats California's Franchise Tax Board for trying to illegally take money - at http://www.livefreenow.org/victories/fls-student-...

It looks like Freedom Law School has helped some people win against the FTB - Freedom Law School, (760) 868-4271 " Guest 123: " I switched my account to a credit union out-of-state who told me they will notify me if they are contacted by the State of California and said they will not cooperate with the State if they attempt to confiscate my funds again."

Read the rest of this PolitiChicks.tv article here: http://politichicks.tv/column/california-tax-boar...

Note: We recommend you read this piece if you can.

CheesyMarch 24, 2012 at 12:24 PM

"Atlas is right - Credit Unions are non-profit, member owned financial institutions that pay more, charge less (or nothing; free checks, free services) and don't act like insufferable swine when you do business with them."

If every eligible person closed their BOA account and joined a CU, it would have an impact. see http://thesilicongraybeard.blogspot.com/2012/03/m...
The more they hassle me, the more I don't want to live in CA, which I don't currently. I have considered getting investment money from CA, and I may. However, the more I hear about the FTB (personally

and in stories online) the more I believe I will make sure any investment money I may take in the future from CA residents will only be earning money in a non-tax state, even if I have to create a corporation for each individual. They are so outrageous they don't even see that they are scaring business and people out of CA. The CA government in general is far too bureaucratic. They do studies on studies on studies. They have people who monitor the red tape, who just create more red tape for yet someone else to monitor. Good old Jerry Brown solved their immediate problems by raising the taxes again. Did he cut out any of the pork fat? No why would he do that?"

Note: This will lead to a revolt of the people. Since Jerry Brown was elected Governor 333,000 business are said to have left California which is incredible if true as we have 34 million people and with seven people in the prototype business we should have about 2.4 million businesses.

David:

I have also heard more threats from the FTB through the rumor mill. However, they have little validity as far as I know. Plus they have committed significant crimes against me under federal law. They can be prosecuted for those much more easily than the FTB could go after me, although they never seem to end posturing. If they make any further attempts to pester me (gone from CA for over 4 years now), I will pursue criminal charges against them; and I am have a much stronger and more recent case than anything they may dream up about me.

Have all the documentation you can muster at hand and be prepared to get some kind of proof you were not where they claim you were or employed as they claim you were as they have shown a proclivity to invent professions, incomes and profits. In my case they invented $10,500 of income for me and it took two years of letter writing, calling my State Assemblyman and Senator's offices as well as my bank, all many times. I must have wasted 100 hours on this and all because I am convinced that our California state government is a criminal enterprise for the profit of the California elected ruling class, their friends and contributors." Note: $10,500 must be one of their favorite figures. That is exactly what they accused me of having not reported to them!

Loren

"Two weeks ago my account was accessed by the FTB for $179 with an additional $150 bank fee for a Court Fee that was paid previously almost 2 years ago. I have all my documents proofing that not only was my fees paid but that the Court had received payment with zero balance. Even though they just pulled out the money again, they still show me owing $179. How are you capable of withdrawing the money yourself but unable to update your own system. The lady I spoke to at the FTB stated, "it probably got sent to the wrong department." Just exactly how does this happen? Let's just keep pulling money out and say they still owe money, no one will even notice!! Come on now."

Note: You can get the bank fee back by threatening to take all your money out and if they refuse go there and do it. It is not a "Court Fee." They make a phone call and they are not a court. They only think they are.

The bank will not let you get out of the door without staying with them after apologizing profusely if you appear there and ask to withraw. They do not want to see this become a common answer to their ways of doing business.

David

"I have recently heard rumors that at least two of the people responsible for abusing me with the FTB were female. The gossip is saying that I have problems with women. As far as I know I do not know either of these women (I never met them). I did not even know they were women.

In my mind this is just another slander on me propagated by the FTB and the gossipmongers. If women at the FTB have played fast and lose with the laws in order to up their performance ratings on tax collecting, they are the ones with the problem.

If they have conspired with some woman that is mad at me for some reason, they are guilty of another felony; and they belong in jail. I am not the one with the problem. They are. I do have problems with some women. I also have problems with some men. I like to think I generally get along well with people.

My impression is that most people find me likable. I do know there have been some men that didn't like me that tried to propagate the slander that I do not get along with women. In other words they try to defame me while deflecting attention to another person or group. I have had many women friends at work; but no I do not automatically like all women, nor do I like all men."

Note: Just because you are paranoid does not mean they are not coming after you. One of our cultural illnesses is that we all want to be liked by everybody and that is not possible so intend to piss somebody off today and you'll have a lot more fun.

Richard:

"l really doubt any of this will be resolved. The FTB is raping people and from what I have read here our banks are holding you in place while the FTB is doing you wrong. I have been fighting them for several years . Unfortunately, I do live in California for over 40+ years. I have never ever owned them any money, but when I didn't file taxes for 07-08-09 they stated accessing my taxes and applying their penalties and interest. Now I am trying to get them to rescind the garnishment action they won't stop even though I sent them everything they wanted including the tax file showing they owe me a return.

Just as a previous poster, when I showed that they taken my money fraudulently, they sent me a form stating that they had sent the IRS a notice that the money they took and I have not received is in the form of a return and is income. Now I will have to pay fines and who knows what because of money they took from me. I don't see where there is any light at the end, only more grief. Where are our rights? Who stands up for us? NO ONE. This is how it ends, no money, on the street, homeless."
Note: It is hard to believe a state bureau could be this evil, but it is.

MOxy:

"My paycheck is currently being garnished $200/pay period due to a $6900 "assessment". I hired a CPA (something I should have done LONG ago, (I know, lesson learned) and it turns out FTB owes ME money. So now I've filed, have to wait the requisite 16 weeks and still have $200 deducted from my paycheck."

Note: Isn't it interesting, and telling, that when they think we owe them money they sweep in like hawks and take it, but when they owe us, we have to wait 16 weeks! This is the arrogance of a tax bureau, Napoleonic power. You are guilty until you prove yourself innocent."

Ernie

"WE ARE ALSO A VICTIM! WE ALREADY PAID OFF OUR TAX BUT FTB IS STILL CALLING! THIS IS TOO MUCH HARRASSMENT!!! CAN WE ALL GET TOGETHER AND FILE A CLASS SUIT VS CALIFORNIA FRANCHISE TAX BOARD? PLEASE ADVISE." Note: That will take a legal foundation and I will be sending copies of this book to several. Let us hope that we can make it happen.

leaveCali:

"Another LLC situation. Our accountant supposedly didn't file the proper documentation that the LLC was closed in 2008, so now they are charging us 8k in taxes plus 5k in penalties for tax year 2009...it is now 2014. 5 years go by before they even give you a word that you have paperwork missing. Criminal Enterprise to say the least."

Note: Shades of Lois Lerner who not only made testimony and then took The Fifth, which abrogates it and why is not the House sticking to the rules, big mistake. Getting away with that emboldened her so she dared to say "The computer ate my emails!" Well "arf!"

Christian Manceras:

"I too just became a victim of this FTB.. I have not lived nor worked in California since 2008. And now they put a block on my account.. And now my payroll check is in limbo because of this... I previously contacted them because they were trying to get me for taxes during my overseas duty in Japan.. Stating that I owe taxes because I lived there.. I called them up and spoke with a representative and told them I wasn't living in California and provided information of my address and proof of this and the representative stated it's our mistake and we will wipe this clean from your record.

After that I thought it was resolved, but I guess not.. I was never given notice about this and had to find out by my bank stating they put a freeze on my account.. I mean do they have such power to do such a thing to people?

They put people into more of a bind so they are unable to get the basic needs of life. Since they froze my account I have getting overdraft fees and can't make a deposit. I am currently in Saudi Arabia working for a Saudi company. Anyone know who I can contact so that I can get this resolved as quickly as possible? I need help urgently... Thanks everyone.. And if anyone is filing a class suit I would like to be part of it.. This branch of government has gone too far and has made so much peoples lives miserable because of it."

Note:

We suggest the California Taxpayers Advocates Office and their number is 800-883-5910, FAX 916-855-2101 They are within the FTB but many have reported getting good results from them.

Christian Miss Dee: In 2002 I left CA. I did not file taxes because I receive Social Security Disability, therefore I am not required to do so. I receive care from my daughter who lives in CA and my parents in Florida.

Over the past year and a half I have spent approximately five months in CA. In 2007 while living in NYC they sent me a letter stating I owed them back taxes for 2002. I called and explained I did not owe and only received $7,400 that year in disability payments. They asked me for a letter of proof from Social Security and told me they would review again. If they find I still owe them they will have me fill out a hardship form which should get approved based on my proof of limited income.

I did not hear back from them until I received a letter

last May 2013. Now they say I owe them back taxes of almost $28,000. Again I called them & was asked for a letter from social security. I complied and did not receive anything from them since. No letters, no phone calls. However, on

December 18th I received a letter from Bank of America stating the FTB has and will take all my funds only for the next 10 business days and that they've assessed a $150 per transaction fee.

So for the two cents literally that I had in my savings account , the other thief, Bank of America, is charging me. What part of the Social Security Act 207 do they both not understand?

I am 100% disabled with a life threatening disease. I struggle each and every month of my life and TONIGHT they will illegally, the two conspirators steal my money, rape me of any possibility of survival, starve me and drive me of my medication which will cause me a set back in my life.

This is America. The Franchise Tax Board of California needs to be stopped. Their employees need to be trained to follow the law and that it is not their job to destroy lives. In 10 days the FTB has destroyed my life.

By January 10th, my two dogs and I will be thrown out of my rented apartment. By January 10th I will be sick because I will not have my needed medication, by January 10th I will be famished because I cannot afford food or gas. By January 15th I will plea to the Lord to take me because the FTB will continue to torture me till death. Leave me alone and put your efforts where the real monies owed can be collected. Leave all of us challenged individuals to live the best way we can with our limitations."

Note: Miss Dee your life is just as important to you as it is to anyone and just as important to anyone else as their humanity obtains. The people of the FTB have no humanity as many of the people with whom they are dealing are needy, hurting and not deserving of their wrath.

Guest 123:

"Freedom Law School beats California's Franchise Tax Board for trying to illegally take money at http://www.livefreenow.org/victories/fls-student-..."
Note: Apparently this is a very helpful organization familiar with what the FTB has been doing. FTB - Freedom Law School (760) 868-4271

Guest 123:

"Protecting your money from further theft" - I found this article that says:

" I switched my account to a credit union out-of-state who told me they will notify me if they are contacted by the State of California and said they will not cooperate with the State if they attempt to confiscate my funds again."

(Read the rest of this PolitiChicks.tv article here: http://politichicks.tv/column/california-tax-boar...)

Note: State Chartered banks, listed and advertising as "State Bank," do not have to and usually will not cooperate with the FTB as everyone in the industry knows what is going on and that Bank of America cooperates with the FTB regularly.

CheesyMarch 24, 2012 at 12:24 PM

"Atlas is right - Credit Unions are non-profit, member owned financial institutions that pay more, charge less (or nothing; free checks, free services) and don't act like insufferable swine when you do business with them.

If every eligible person closed their BOA account and joined a Credit Union, it would have an impact. see http://thesilicongraybeard.blogspot.com/2012/03/m...

Note: Yes it would and I got an immediate rescission of my charge by threatening to close my account the next day when this first happened to me.

David:

"The more they hassle me, the more I don't want to live in CA, which I don't currently. I have considered getting investment money from CA, and I may. However, the more I hear about the FTB (personally and in stories online) the more I believe I will make sure any investment money I may take in the future from CA residents will only be earning money in a non-tax state, even if I have to create a corporation for each individual.

They are so outrageous they don't even see that they are scaring business and people out of CA. The CA government in general is far too bureaucratic. They do studies on studies on studies. They have people who monitor the red tape, who just create more red tape for yet someone else to monitor. Good old Jerry Brown solved their immediate problems by raising the taxes again. Did he cut out any of the pork fat? No why would he do that?"

Note: Over 333,000 businesses have left California since Governor Brown was elected. By his reckoning things are going very well. By the state Controller they are not. Now whom should we believe?

David:

"I have also heard of more threats from the FTB through the rumor mill. However, they have little validity as far as I know. Plus they have committed significant crimes against me under federal law. They can be prosecuted for those much more easily than the FTB could go after me, although they never seem to end posturing. If they make any further attempts to pester me (gone from CA for over four years now), I will pursue criminal charges against them; and I am have a much stronger and more recent case than anything they may dream up about me."

Note:

Criminal charges can only be brought by a District Attorney or a State Attorney General and you can certainly present your case to them and get action unless they too have gone over to the dark side.

Reply

"WOW, I am astonished at the posts here. I thought I had it bad. Is anyone able to answer how can the FTB operate in complete disregard to the Constitutions and more importantly due process? How can the legislature give an entity powers that are above the law?

If the FTB can be given powers above the law why can't other law enforcement be given similar powers? Why can't a narcotics detective be given the same powers? We accuse you of dealing drugs. A hearing will be held in 30 days at which time you have do show you are not dealing drugs. Failure to show you aren't or failure to respond and you will be sentenced for the allegation. People our country is far down the slippery slope of tyranny."

Note: Law enforcement should not bother us as they know the criminal law and are sworn to "keep the peace." The danger comes in bureaucrats who are now being armed and put in the field with no training and they go nuts with their power. The recent Stanford Study has again shown us how easy it is to take ordinary people and make junior Gestapo officers of them."

Loren:

"Two weeks ago my account was accessed by the FTB for $179 with an additional $150 bank fee for a Court Fee that was paid previously almost two years ago. I have all my documents proving that not only were my fees paid but that the Court had received payment producing zero balance. Even though they just pulled out the money again, they still show me owing $179. How are you capable of withdrawing the money yourself but unable to update your own system? The lady I spoke to at the FTB stated, "it probably got sent to the wrong department." Just exactly how does this happen? Let's just keep pulling money out and say they still owe money, no one will even notice!! Come on now."

Note:

Sounds like another Lois Lerner syndrome here.... David: "I have recently heard rumors that at least two of the people responsible for abusing me with the FTB were female. The gossip is saying that I have problems with women. As far as I know I do not know either of these women (I never met them). I did not even know they were women. In my mind this is just another slander on me propagated by the FTB and the gossipmongers. If women at the FTB have played fast and lose with the laws in order to up their performance ratings on tax collecting, they are the ones with the problem.

If they have conspired with some woman that is mad at me for some reason, they are guilty of another felony; and they belong in jail. I am not the one with the problem. They are. I do have problems with some women. I also have problems with some men. I like to think I generally get along well with people.

My impression is that most people find me likable. I do know there have been some men that didn't like me that tried to propagate the slander that I do not get along with women. In other words they try to defame me while deflecting attention to another person or group. I have had many women friends at work; but no I do not automatically like all women, nor do I like all men."

Note: Just because you are paranoid does not mean they are not coming after you!

Richard:

"l really doubt any of this will be resolved. The FTB is raping people and from what I have read here our banks are holding you in place while the FTB is doing you wrong. I have been fighting them for several years . Unfortunately, I do live in California for over 40+ years. I have never ever owned them any money, but when I didn't file taxes for 07-08-09 they stated assessing my taxes and applying their penalties and interest. Now I am trying to get them to rescind the garnishment action they won't stop even though I sent them everything they wanted including the tax file showing they owe me a return.

Just as a previous poster, when I showed that they had taken my money fraudulently, they sent me a form stating that they had sent the IRS a notice that the money they took and I have not received is in the form of a return and is income. Now I will have to pay fines and who knows what because of money they took from me. I don't see where there is any light at the end, only more grief. Where are our rights? Who stands up for us? NO ONE. This is how it ends, no money, on the street, homeless."

Note: It is a serious mistake not to file even if you cannot pay. What you do in that case is seal the debt and document your forthrightness. By not filing you not only leave the meter running, so to speak, but you incur a big, fat fine to boot.

MOxy:

"My paycheck is currently being garnished $200/pay period due to a $6,900 "assessment". I hired a CPA (something I should have done LONG ago, I know, lesson learned) and it turns out FTB owes ME money. So now I've filed, have to wait the requisite 16 weeks and still have $200 deducted from my paycheck."
Note: Is it any news they work the rules to their favor? Never forget with whom you are dealing with in the California Franchise Tax Board.
Ernie;

"WE ARE ALSO A VICTIM! WE ALREADY PAID OFF OUR TAX BUT FTB IS STILL CALLING! THIS IS TOO MUCH HARRASSMENT!!! CAN WE ALL GET TOGETHER AND FILE A CLASS SUIT VS CALIFORNIA FRANCHISE TAX BOARD? PLEASE ADVISE....
Note: Again, this will take a legal foundation and I have not found one yet, but hope this publication will do it.

LeaveCali:

"Another LLC situation. Our accountant supposedly didn't file the proper documentation that our LLC was closed in 2008, so now they are charging us 8k in taxes plus 5k in penalties for tax year 2009. It is now 2014. Five years go by before they even give you a word that you have paperwork missing. Criminal Enterprise to say the least."

Note:

This should be your accountant's responsibility, but we have had trouble with them too. Some are good; some are not, but you may get in touch with the FTB and ask them to stick it to the accountant.

Lisette:

"For those of you who haven't already done so, I would recommend contacting the FTB Taxpayer Advocacy hotline like someone else mentioned.

I admittedly and wrongly thought that the CA FTB processed late returns with no penalty where a refund is due like the IRS. Lesson learned on my part. I voluntarily filed my 2011 and 2012 returns about a month ago. When I called the FTB earlier this week to ensure they had received my returns. They didn't have any record and transferred me to what I thought was another department. The individual I spoke with very condescendingly informed me that not only would I not receive a refund but that I owed them over $4,000 for tax year 2011 and that they had already informed my employer of a 25% levy of my wages effective 2/21/14. I was completely shocked. He explained that I owed interest and penalties but after going in circles I couldn't understand how interest could be charged on a zero balance. The only thing he would do for me was to modify the levy to $185 per pay period. He then informed me that interest would continue to accrue and the levy would remain in place until they processed my return which could take six months and that if they determined that an overpayment was made on my part, they would send me a check. I offered to fax a copy my return but he refused to accepted it stating that they only accept faxed returns if the FTB owes the taxpayer a refund.

Last night I googled information on FTB levies and found that there is a Taxpayer Advocate hotline. I called today and after only a one minute explanation of my issue I was informed that what I had been told yesterday was incorrect. She shared with me that I was speaking to a collection agent and that they often give misleading and incorrect information. She asked me to fax a copy of my return and promised to call me back after reviewing it. As promised, she called me back about an hour later and informed me that she had contacted my employer to stop the levy. When I asked her how much of a penalty I would owe and she said nothing, they owe me a refund. To be honest I didn't even care about the refund at that point, I was just grateful not to owe any money.

You can find the Taxpayer Advocacy phone number on the CA FTB website. Hope this helps someone."

Note:

You have been very helpful and the California FTB Taxpayer Advocates Office is at 800 883 5910. You can FAX them letters and documents at 916-855-5910. The FAX does not give you a callback.

Donnie:

"The FTB levied my bank accounts also. I haven't called them yet out of stark raving fear..! If anyone has that much power to just ruin a person for state revenue, think about what else they can do! Anyway, I've worked up the courage to confront the matter because I'm on the verge of being homeless over all this.

I was unemployed (still am) when they levied me without any of the normal (Calif DUE PROCESS). The State of California must be really desperate to chop it own nose off to spite its face. These action not only hurts the state, is hurts the economy.! This level of draconian measures to generate revenue appears to be out of "desperation". When any "entity" starts to treat its symbiotic circle with such degree of impunity.. That could mean one thing...

A California Financial Implosion...

There has to be a better way to receive tax revenue from "regular people" who make under 70 grand a year.?!?! We're not millionaires here, just the people who power the economy."
Note: Well said and we are dealing with a schizophrenic bureau that acts like it was operating in France where you are guilty until you prove yourself innocent. That is not America, much as the elected ruling class wants it to be. Call the Taxpayer Advocates number listed above. They appear to be the last vestige of sanity in the California state government.

Luis:

"Boy do I have a good one for you guys! It all started back in 2011 I was 19, young and reckless. I got pulled over for speeding, running a stop sign, and not wearing a seatbelt. Before I could go to court I was arrested for an unrelated matter and sentenced to four months in county jail. It was the county's responsibility to get me to my court date. They didn't take me and I was found guilty in absentia and had a failure to appear imposed. Upon my release I immediately set up a court date for that matter. This is where things get good!

I told the judge my plight and she just looked at me and said "you should have taken care of business" and dismissed me. I then received a letter from the courts saying I had to pay them $1100 immediately in full. I didn't have the means to do so and when I tried to set up a payment plan they said no so said screw them!

A couple months went by then I got a letter from AllianceOne repeating what the courts had said. I called and tried to set up a payment plan and again I was denied... I finally got my stuff together and was working at a temp agency to provide for my daughter and girlfriend. This time I didn't get a letter. All I got was a really small paycheck I only made about 500 a week but my check came out to about 200! I called the office and asked if there was some kind of mistake and she said no you're wages are being garnished by the FTB and gave me a number to call. I called and was told I still owed 1200, I had to beg the lady to lower my garnishment from 50% to 10% I told her two people depended on me to feed them, I'm lucky she had a heart. Here comes the good part.

I was hired by the company I was temping at permanently and garnishment stopped! I was so relieved but I knew it was only temporary so I sat and waited but the day never came instead they sent me another letter saying this time I owed 1800! I didn't even bother calling I gave up. I had a chance at an apprenticeship doing pipefitting but when I went to the DMV to renew my license the good old FTB had placed a hold on my license. And they intercepted my California refund check to top it off! Cold hearted monsters is what they are. All this for $1800? I smell desperation these guys need to be knocked down off their high horse IMHO!"

Note:

You have hit on the key to the whole problem: The Democrats in the California legislature love to spend other people's money and they are in charge, if they can keep their people out of jail. Three are now under felony indictments! Your case has some extra spin, but it fits the picture."

john h:

"Hah.. I moved from California to Arizona, registered my truck in Arizona, two years later the FTB took $700 out of my account for DMV fees when I didn't live in the state! I finally got it back, but typical of FTB ripping you off."

Note: The FTB is getting away with much of this because some banks are cooperating with them, particularly the Bank of America. Put your money in a state chartered bank after asking if they cooperate with orders from the FTB, which is not a court and they should not cooperate with them. Texas 2014

"My bank account was just levied on Valentines Day.

For alleged taxes owed in 2002. My tax preparer gave me a copy of my 2002 Income tax forms which I signed and mailed 30 days before the due date. My bank that I wrote the check from found my bank statement in 2003 showing the check number amount and cleared date. They do not have a copy of the actual cleared check because it was 12 years ago.

FTB claims I filed my 2002 taxes 14 months late and that I never paid.

They said I filed my 2003 taxes on time and got a refund for it. So tell me, how did they get my 2003 taxes before my 2002 taxes and process a refund if they claim I still owed from the previous year.

Who the Hell cashed my check then?

I'm in bureaucracy hell with the FTB right now and am seeking an attorney to sue the state of California. I have a 20 year history of paying bills and taxes in full and early every single working year of my life. Because they are going back 12 years, the FTB knows no bank has the actual checks from that far back. Depending on the state where your bank account is at, the laws can be different. I paid my 2002 taxes in March 2003 and all I have to prove it is the bank statement and my personal copy of my check ledger.

What the FTB is doing is wrong. If anyone has paid their taxes on time but is still being penalized or levied, please post if you have an attorney trying to get a class action going."

Note: It sounds like you had sufficient records from the bank in the first round. They were way beyond the four year statute of limitations on the matter in the first case. An attorney on this matter is very expensive overkill and they love it when you do that as they can run up your bill at will, and believe it; they will." Kelly: "Just happened to me. I signed onto my banking app to deposit a check and found $1000 missing from my savings.I got the documents for the fund hold from my bank stating it's for taxes owed from 2007. I was in trade school for the first three and a half months of 2007 then moved directly to Utah for work. I earned exactly ZERO dollars while I was in California. I tried calling the number my bank gave me and was on hold for a full hour before I had to hangup because I needed to get back to work. IMO this is typical California government thievery. When I left California it was to find work in my field and with every intention to move back in a couple years but after comparing the laws and practices of California against another state I don't think I'll ever go back. Which is sad because most of my family and many friends still live there."

Note: 330,000 businesses and many millions of people have left California since the Democrats have been in the majority. Who knows where this will end? It appears the state, if not the nation, will have to collapse before the large mass of voters figure out Democrats are the problem. Richard Anderson "On January 13, 2012 FTB issued an Order to Withhold because of a Tax Debt for the year 2008. The Fi)Bank of Stockton) froze my entire account so I had absolutely no money to live on.

On 5/1/2011 Financial Institutions were required to perform an account audit to determine if there are Protected Federal Benefits. My income consists of VA Benefits/SSDI/Disability CIV Serv. All of these agencies under 31 CFR 212 are deemed protected federal benefits.

42 USC 407 has protected Social Security for a very long time and 31 CFR 212 clarifies and requires that Financial Institutions perform the account audit within two business days and set a protected amount as determined by a 60 day look-back period to a) give me reasonable and customary access to my protected accounts. Instead the Bank of Stockton froze my account and at that point I would have done just about anything because we were hungry.

The FI should have filled out part and not satisfied the order. 31 CFR 212.5/6 offers safe haven to FI's that perform the account audit and states that the FI is in violation of Federal Laws if they do not comply with the terms of 31 CFR 212.

FTB then told me, or coerced me, to sign a contract for the tax debt and basically said I would have no access to my account until I signed the thing. I felt at the time this was the only alternative.

I have been disputing this issue with the FI because had it not been for them I would not have been in this position today. The FTB knows the law and also preys on the folks that are rendered destitute because of their actions.

FTB is smart though because they know they are off the hood and in this case since I was not entirely aware of the law I will lose about $15,000 by the time it is paid off.

The financial institution insists they have no obligation to protect because the Order to Withhold is not a garnishment order per se.

31 CFR 212 is supposed to stop the illegal practice of freezing accounts of the aged/disabled leaving them penniless and willing to do just about anything to access their funds. And thus I signed a pact with the devil. 31 CFR 212 prohibits banks from charging what is called an impermissible fee. It is against the law to charge against an account which contains protected federal benefits. If more than one person is involved I see conspiracy to commit federal crimes.

The law is the law and the FI is playing dumb. I could use some advice. I know I am right but need to jerk this banks chain.

The attorney for the FI is just toying with me and I think they feel that they will prevail because I will give up.

Social Security can only be garnished for back child support from a state child support agency or the federal government. IRS can levy 15 per cent of income only. State tax agencies have no authority to freeze accounts with federally protected benefits. Even the IRS frowns on the practice of freezing accounts with Social Security and VA Benefits. VA Benefits have been protected since 1935 and SSI since 1940.

42 USC 407 protects SSI from garnishment at the source and 42 USC 207 protects the income where it is deposited.

Under 31 CFR 212 the account holder does not have to exert anything to protect because ACH indicates that your benefits are protected by placing XX in the name of the depositing entity. it looks like this on your statement: XXSOCSEC or XXVABENE or SSCIVSERV. That means that the agency is telling the bank to lay off. XX means exempt.

I do not have the funds to get a $1000 an hour

attorney so I am stuck and frustrated fighting this guy; not gaining or losing but a simple phone call from a real lawyer would help me so much but so far I am still alone in my fight.

The Bank of Stiockton ordered the closing of my account but that would have caused even more financial hardship and I plead with them to keep it open because I was disabled. They retaliated instead of admitting they were wrong.

Protected Government Benefits are considered property and therefore protected under the 14th amendment. The Supremacy Clause was broken when the did not extend due process instead they went in and froze my account with no warrant. The 4th amendment I believe states that they can take what is mentioned in the warrant or in this case the Order to Withhold. FTB is specific and asks for ALL but then describes the account types. There is no mention of Federal Protected Benefits because it is against the law to levy them.

Further the State of California further protects you against creditors by granting an automatic, in my case, at the time of $2875 a month plus the protected amount that should be determined when the account audit was done.

The Bank failed miserably and sticks to its position that the FTB told them to freeze my account. I maintain that since the agency has deemed my money protected and the bank has the ability either automatically or mamually to see the XX that they are liable to me. I would have loved to get the FTB but they are way to slippery and has a very short statute of limitations."

Note:

You have the law well in hand and can make an excellent presentation to the FTB Advocacy Unit we have mentioned many times, but you should also get in touch with your State Senator, Assemblyperson and Congressional Representative as they all have responsibilities in the areas you have so well documented here.

Christine:

"I was on active duty and was stationed in CA for approximately two years. I was never a legal resident of CA. Therefore, I was not required to pay taxes. I filed taxes normally with an accountant from the Navy. Ten years later, I receive a notice from the state indicating that I did not pay taxes to them. I was never a resident, legally! How is this just? I was serving this great country and now this stat that I have no affiliation with is threatening to take my hard earned money. I am contacting a lawyer!"

Note: I recommend you contact The California

Taxpayers Advocates Office and their number is 800-883-5910, FAX 916-855-2101 and they will help you. They are the one sane unit in that bureaucracy. Gerry Christine:

"Contact the California Taxpayer's Advocate Office and they'll straighten this out for you. They stepped in and made the FTB give me back all the money they had stolen from by bank accounts. They are truly the "good guys." Woz: "The FTB must not levy or garnish any money in any account designated to receive SS benefits, as it is protected under Social Security Act §207.

Social Security Act Section 207 clearly prohibits and restricts all debtors including a State against the use of any levy or garnishments to reach social security benefits.

FTB is in violation of the U.S. Supreme Court 1/10/73 ruling, "Doris Philpott and Wm. Wilkes v. Essex County Welfare Board, 409 U.S," and that these paid benefits do not lose their exempt status, even when you cash the checks or have been "paid" in a lump sum into a bank account.

Look up the facts and arguments yourself and then decide.

I might suggest that you ask your state representatives, your state senators, your US

Representatives, your US Senators, a well-qualified individual to champion the cause to correct a wrong, to push for legislation that will positively change the existing unfair and unethical collection practices of the FTB and other overly aggressive debt collectors.

In short, let us mobilize and push for positive changes. Let us all work within the legislative process to bring about positive changes.

Good day and good luck to all."

Note:

All "spot-on" recommendations from experience. FTB Retaliation: "I can trump most of these, unfortunately. I was forced to file bankruptcy in late 2013; it was approved in March 2014. Nine days later the FTB Criminal Investigation Division showed up in my office unannounced (I wasn't there) scared my staff, and then later that day (when I had a lawyer contact them), refused to tell my lawyer what is was regarding: "Oh, He Knows!" - that's a direct quote. That was Tuesday. Friday night at 5:00 p.m. I was Arrested.

They filed Felony Tax Evasion charges under R&TC 19706! When contacted the DA said "They don't think he intended to pay" WHICH IS NOT A CLAIM UNDER 19706.

Under 19701(c) they must show Willful (defined as e.g., "evil") Intent; because we don't throw people with debt in jail. The DA IMMEDIATELY offered a plea of misdemeanor "late filing" if I agreed to pay."

HOW IS NOT A SHAKEDOWN?

Note: This is the most frightening post of all as it shows the FTB's willingness to access the criminal-justice system for their purposes and in ways consistent with Napoleonic law that is not that under which we live. Our law extends from English Common Law in which we are innocent until the state proves us guilty. The FTB is operating the other way around and that is unconstitutional federally and by the state."

Butch Hurtin:

"Nineteen years after I moved from California they seized my bank account for my last partial year there and they have added in penalties and interest ten amounting to ten times the few hundred dollars they said I owed for that tax year.

These bastards are using all ex-citizens as pawns and violating federal law. They need to be exposed in a television commercial which will cost them more in tourism and respect. I will donate to the production. I have already written to the AARP and Readers Digest to do a story on the California con. They will not even settle for half of what is owed when it is all interest and penalties."

Note: You need to get in touch with the Advocacy Unit, your old State Senator and Assemblyperson as well your Congressperson as they are in violation of both the state and federal constitutions. Forget AARP and Readers Digest. They have both gone hard left.

Ismael Luis Perez:

"Put me right in there. Even after describing my hardships, they still wiped my accounts clean. They are behaving as if one has not paid taxes at all."

Greg Smith:

"Just happened to me too! I left CA in 2008 after living there my entire life - went to Texas to escape all the liberal bull crap and idiotic government decisions. I went online to check my bank balance and there was a hold on my checking and savings accounts (with significant cash in both). I called my bank immediately and they told me it was a CA FTB levy and gave me their phone number. I contacted them and no one could tell me why the levy had been placed! Seriously?

They faxed the release over to my bank and it took 24 hours to release and my bank charged me $100. I am sending them a letter asking for reimbursement, but I really want to ask for money for my time and a fraudulent levy put on my personal assets. Has anyone consulted an attorney with regards to this fraud yet??? Thanks y'all - from the wonderful State of Texas!!!"

Note:

California has been running on sunshine and old Beach Boys songs too long, but they are getting their come-uppance as 333,000 businesses and millions of people have left the state since the Democrats took over.

Tannerlove:

"I just got a wage garnishment for a ticket they say I didn't pay in 1997 for expired registration that is now $1797.00!!!! They say there is nothing I can do, when I asked the person at the "FTB" why it took them 17 years!!!!! she said, "our company" just got this in 2013!!!!! They never suspended my license, I certainly can't come up with a receipt from 1997.......this is CRAZY!!!" Note: No one has to say "statute of limitations," "failure to execute" or "irresponsible administration" to define this case. They are written all over this one. Tzeigler: "They levied me over $55000, yes thousand, because of an old high interest

I lost several thousand dollars trying to keep paying and ultimately lost property because they assumed that I was making almost a million dollars when actually I had zero income for the past five years. You think they would go after the corrupt mortgage company that got rich off illegal "liar loans."

May 3, 2014 at 7:24 am Ranchingmama: Got me too. They took my entire savings of $25,000.00 and over half of my checking."

Butch Hurtin:

"Yes, Nineteen years after I moved from California they seized my bank account for my last partial year there and they have added in penalties and interest ten amounting to ten times the few hundred dollars they said I owed for that tax year.

These bastards are using all ex-citizens as pawns and violating federal law. They need to be exposed in a television commercial which will cost them more in tourism and respect. I will donate to the production. I have already written to the AARP and Readers Digest to do a story on the California con. They will not even settle for half of what is owed when it is all interest and penalties."

Note: What we really need is a Federal action to uphold the Constitutional provision that no state can collect a tax in another and that in no case are taxing authorities allowed to operate under Napoleonic law when ours is based on English Common Law wherein the accused is innocent until the state proves him guilty. The IRS and FTB operate the other way around: If they say you owe them they feel righteous in taking your money because you have not proven to them that you did not owe. The fact that you were totally unaware of the matter makes no difference to them: They are despots by definition.

Anonymous:

"California is broke and will use any means necessary to plunder private citizens savings and retirement to cover the costs of decades of failed government policies.

California has nearly quadrupled the number of traffic tickets it issues annually from just a few years ago; coincidence!? I think not! The real war is between government workers and private citizens. They will do anything to keep their government paychecks and bloated pension funds. Anyone in the private sector going to get a pension from their employer?"

Note: Your points are all valid: California is more than broke; it is in a bottomless pit and digging. They apparently feel this justifies taking our money at will. Or, as Rush Limbaugh says, "It's their money, dummy!"

Any government employee has about a 20% to 30% advantage over any private sector employee because he cannot be fired so the banks will lend to him when they will not to we who work in the private sector, and they have pension plans that net them 60% to 150% of their last year's salaries. They do not have to plan or save for old age; it is done for them and richly. So, they rag on us for all the money we make?"

FTB Retaliation:

"I can trump most of these, unfortunately. I was forced to file bankruptcy in late 2013; it was approved in March 2014. Nine Days later the FTB Criminal Investigation Division showed up in my office unannounced (I wasn't there) scared my staff, and then later that day (when I had a lawyer contact them), they refused to tell my lawyer what is was regarding: "Oh, He Knows!" – that's a direct quote. That was Tuesday. Friday night at 5:00 p.m. I was Arrested.

They filed Felony Tax Evasion charges under R&TC 19706. When contacted the DA said "They don't think he intended to pay" WHICH IS NOT A CLAIM UNDER 19706.

Under 19701(c) they must show Willful (defined as e.g., "evil") Intent; because we don't throw people with debt in jail. The DA IMMEDIATELY offered a plea of misdemeanor "late filing" if I agreed to pay. HOW IS NOT A SHAKEDOWN?"

Note: That is exactly what it is, but you have to understand that these are people who apparently have felt small and powerless all their lives. They got a state job and are told of all their power so they get carried away and start making things up to inflate their flat egos."

Adrian Vance:

"I again thank you all for continuing to post your stories here. I have apparently beaten them back, in my case, but it took a lot of time in document searching, calling the FTB, IRS and Bank of America. It appears that you have to make so much noise and generate so much trouble that your case becomes a losing situation to them and they are paying more in bureau time than they could get from you, but they never give you a final document of closure of any kind. They just leave it hanging and that is the worst part as we can only imagine they will be attacking our estates after we are gone and your executor is probably your child, inexperienced in these matters and ready just to give them the money to get rid of them. These people are truly evil and now we find the IRS is doing it too. How long will it be before

America is in total rebellion?"

Woz:

"The FTB must not levy or garnish any money in any account designated to receive SS benefits, as it is protected under Social Security Act §207.
Social Security Act Section 207 clearly prohibits and restricts all debtors including a State against the use of any levy or garnishments to reach social security benefits.

FTB is in violation of the U.S. Supreme Court 1/10/73 ruling, "Doris Philpott and Wm. Wilkes v. Essex County Welfare Board, 409 U.S," and that these paid benefits do not lose their exempt status, even when you cash the checks or have been "paid" in a lump sum into a bank account.
Look up the facts and arguments yourself and then decide.

I might suggest that you ask your state representatives, your state senators, your US Representatives, your US Senators, a well-qualified individual to champion the cause to correct a wrong, to push for legislation that will positively change the existing unfair and unethical collection practices of the FTB and other overly aggressive debt collectors.

In short, let us mobilize and push for positive changes. Let us all work within the legislative process to bring about positive changes. Good day and good luck to all."

Note: Woz is spot on with all points he notes. The FTB took over $800 from the checking account where my SSI benefit is deposited and had to return it. I do have other earnings deposited there, which some say takes that protection away, but the amount is low as they are all old book royalties and probably do not exceed $1,000 per year.

Gerry Christine:

"Contact the California Taxpayer's Advocate Office and they'll straighten this out for you. They stepped in and made the FTB give me back all the money they had stolen from by bank accounts. They are truly the "good guys."

Note: We have previously mentioned this group and they are at: California Taxpayers Advocates Office and their numbers are 800-883-5910 and FAX 916-855-2101

Richard Anderson:

"On January 13, 2012 FTB issued an Order to Withhold because of a Tax Debt for the year 2008. The Financial Bank of Stockton froze my entire account so I had absolutely no money to live on.

On 5/1/2011 Financial Institutions were required to perform an account audit to determine if there are Protected Federal Benefits. My income consists of VA Benefits/SSDI/Disability CIV Serv. All of these agencies under 31 CFR 212 are deemed protected federal benefits.
42 USC 407 has protected Social Security for a very long time and 31 CFR 212 clarifies and requires that Financial Institutions perform the account audit within 2 business days and set a protected amount as determined by a 60 day look-back period to a) give me reasonable and customary access to my protected accounts.

Instead the Bank of Stockton froze my account and at that point I would have done just about anything because we were hungry. The bank should have not executed the order. 31 CFR 212.5/6 offers safe haven to FI's that perform the account audit and states that the FI is in violation of Federal Laws if they do not comply with the terms of 31 CFR 212.

The FTB then coerced me to sign a contract for the tax debt and said I would have no access to my account until I signed the thing. I felt at the time this was the only alternative.

I have been disputing this issue with the FI because had it not been for them I would not have been in this position today. The FTB knows the law and also preys on the folks that are rendered destitute because of their actions.

FTB is smart though because they know they are off the hook and in this case since I was not entirely aware of the law I will lose about $15,000 by the time it is paid off.

The financial institution insists they have no obligation to protect because the Order to Withhold is not a garnishment order per se. 31 CFR 212 is supposed to stop the illegal practice of freezing accounts of the aged and disabled leaving them penniless and willing to do just about anything to access their funds.

I signed a pact with the devil: 31 CFR 212 prohibits banks from charging what is called an impermissable fee. It is against the law to charge against an account which contains protected federal benefits. If more than one person is involved I see conspiracy to commit federal crimes.

The law is the law and the FI is playing dumb. I could use some advise. I know I am right but need to jerk this banks chain. The attorney for the FI is just toying with me and I think they feel that they will prevail because I will give up.

Social Security can only be garnished for back child support from a state child support agency or the federal government. IRS can levy 15 per cent of income only. State tax agencies have no authority to freeze accounts with federal protected benefits. Even the IRS frowns on the practice of freezing accounts with Social Security and VA Benefits. VA Benefits have been protected since 1935 and SSI since 1940.

2 USC 407 protects SSI from garnishment at the source and 42 USC 207 protects the income where it is deposited.

Under 31 CFR 212 the account holder does not have to exert anything to protect because ACH indicates that your benefits are protected by placing XX in the name of the depositing entity. it looks like this on your statement: XXSOCSEC or XXVABENE or SSCIVSERV. That means that the agency is telling the bank to lay off. XX means exempt.

I do not have the funds to get a 1000 an hour attorney so I am stuck frustrated fighting this guy and not gaining or losing but a simple phone call from a real lawyer would help me so much but so far I am still alone in my fight. The Bank of Stockton ordered the closing of my account but that would have caused even more financial hardship and I plead with them to keep it open because I was disabled. They retaliated instead of admitting they were wrong.

Protected Government Benefits are considered property and therefore protected under the 14th amendment. The Supremacy Clause was broken when the did not extend due process instead they went in and froze my account with no warrant. The 4th amendment I believe states that they can take what is mentioned in the warrant or in this case the Order to Withhold. FTB is specific and asks for ALL but then describes the account types. There is no mention of Federal Protected Veteran Benefits because it is against the law to levy them.

Further the State of California further protects you against creditors by granting an automatic in my case at the time of $2,875 a month plus the protected amount that should be determined when the account audit was done.

The Bank failed miserably and sticks to its position that the FTB told them to freeze my account. I maintain that since the agency has deemed my money protected and the bank has the ability either automatically or manually to see the XX that they are liable to me. I would have loved to get the FTB but they are way too slippery and has a very short statute of limitations."

Note: All valid information and you should contact every elected official in your district, county, state and federal as these FTB crimes slice through every jurisdiction all the way to Washington. I do not think that an attorney can do anything for you that you cannot do for yourself in a matter of this kind.

March 26, 2014 at 3:49 pm

Citizen: "Any government worker that hides behind their job as justification for what they do is a domestic terrorist by any definition. The media will call you a terrorist, but Americans and your children will call you a patriot! You can do something or just whine about it."

Note:

Appropriate viewpoint and if we all impinged on our elected people we would not have these problems as they are funding these bureaus. If the bureaus don't behave they can just shut off the money and the bureau dies.

Anonymous "The CA FTB has it coming. It only takes a handful of martyrs to make an example out of a corrupt government. I'm letting them steam roll over me, but I'll have the last laugh. For every dollar they take from me, it will one day cost them a million. We empower our government to wage war for liberty and freedom, now and again we have to wage war against our government to keep those liberties and freedom. They know where we live, but we know where they work! You can continue to kick the can down the road and let your children endure the same tyranny, or you can lay down your life and make an example out of a corrupt government. If they take away your ability to survive, then take away theirs too!"

Note: I was not quite sure where you were going with your comment, Anonymous as you were "...letting them steam roller over me," and I am not too sure how that will get you "...the last laugh," unless they have tickling rubber fingers on the steamroller. What we are advocating here is that everyone affected by these criminals should document their cases to their elected representatives at the state and federal level as laws and two or three Constitutions are being violated in these confiscations. It has to stop and people have to go to jail for this for to end "once and forever."

Texas Tee: "Just happened to me too! I left CA in 2008 after living there my entire life - went to Texas to escape all the liberal bull crap and idiotic government decisions. I went online to check my bank balance and there was a hold on my checking and savings accounts (with significant cash in both). I called my bank immediately and they told me it was a CA FTB levy and gave me their phone number. I contacted them and no one could tell me why the levy had been placed! Seriously? They faxed the release over to my bank and it took 24 hours to release and my bank charged me $100. I am sending them a letter asking for reimbursement, but I really want to ask for money for my time and a fraudulent levy put on my personal assets. Has anyone consulted an attorney with regards to this fraud yet??? Thanks y'all - from the wonderful State of Texas!!!"

Note: This is becoming a common refrain. Where we know how much we spend educating our people, what they earn and what they pay in taxes, this is a loss that is in the billions where millions of workers have left the state.

Kathie Tannerlove:

"I just got a wage garnishment for a ticket. They say I didn't pay in 1997 for expired registration that is now $1797.00! They say there is nothing I can do, when I asked the person at the "FTB" why it took them 17 years! She said, "our company" just got this in 2013!!!!! They never suspended my license, I certainly can't come up with a receipt from 1997. This is crazy!

Note: You should not have to come up with a receipt from 1997 as there is a four year statute of limitations on matters of this kind, but the IRS and FTB have the idea they are above the law and their regulations prevail. Their regulations are Napoleonic, you are guilty until you prove your innocence. This alone makes the entire taxing structure of the bureaus unconstitutional."

Brave Dave: Is anyone looking onto a class-action lawsuit against the FTB? Any attorneys involved? Email me at oedtrex at yahoo dot com" Note: We are hoping to interest a legal foundation in this issue and cases. We feel a class action is not only indicated, but a virtual "slam-dunk!" Of course we are going up against the establishment and their judges so if nothing else we will prove the complete corruption of our government.

Adam:

"They keep liquidating my bank account. No money to support my wife and kid. I was not a resident nor ever rented or owned property there. My parents did and 14 years of this is unreal. They will not answer straight and cannot keep taking all of my money. How can they put families in this position?"Note: This post, like so many here, show the utter inhumanity of this bureau, and we have read of similar actions by the IRS with the capper being the middle-western family they evicted from their home as they were sitting down to Christmas Eve dinner. Four children were involved in that case. What are they going to think of government all their lives? They will never forget that incident.

In Summation

The California Franchise Tax board is an evil organization operating at the pleasure of the Governor of California and the legislature, but it is the Governor who has the oversight responsibility. We have appraised him of our case and have been told by FTB people that he did respond specifically to them regarding my case and they relented, but refused to give me a final, closing letter. Apparently, they want me to worry that my mailbox will have another one of their duns some day. These are evil people.

Adrian Vance